Sleeping with Bread

Holding What Gives You Life

Dennis Linn
Sheila Fabricant Linn
Matthew Linn, S.J.

ILLUSTRATIONS BY FRANCISCO MIRANDA

Paulist Press Mahwah/New York

Acknowledgments

We wish to thank the following persons for their time and loving care in reading the manuscript for this book and offering suggestions: Rev. Robert Faricy, S.J.; Barbara and Dr. Morton Kelsey; Dr. Ken, Sheren, Naomi and Alayna Larsen; Maria Maggi; Rev. Robert Sears, S.J.; Rev. Leo Thomas, O.P.; Dr. Diana Villegas.

Book Design by Saija Autrand, Faces Type & Design.

IMPRIMI POTEST:
Bert Thelen, S.J.
Provincial, Wisconsin Province of the Society of Jesus
September 29, 1994

Library of Congress Cataloging-in-Publication Data

Linn, Dennis.
    Sleeping with bread : holding what gives you life / by Dennis Linn, Sheila Fabricant Linn, Matthew Linn.
       p. cm.
    Includes bibliographical references.
    ISBN 0-8091-3579-5
    1. Christian life. 2. Faith. 3. Spiritual direction. 4. Spiritual formation. 5. Linn, Dennis.
  I. Linn, Sheila Fabricant. II. Linn, Matthew. III. Title.
    BV4501.2.L546 1995
    248.4'6—dc20   95-2305
                                                              CIP

Published by Paulist Press
997 Macarthur Boulevard
Mahwah, N.J. 07430

www.paulistpress.com

Printed and bound in Mexico

We gratefully dedicate this book to

Jim & Mary Jo Brauner

Maria Maggi

George & Mary Ann Schmidt

who have so often given us the bread we needed each day.

Sleeping with Bread

During the bombing raids of World War II, thousands of children were orphaned and left to starve. The fortunate ones were rescued and placed in refugee camps where they received food and good care. But many of these children who had lost so much could not sleep at night. They feared waking up to find themselves once again homeless and without food. Nothing seemed to reassure them. Finally, someone hit upon the idea of giving each child a piece of bread to hold at bedtime. Holding their bread, these children could finally sleep in peace. All through the night the bread reminded them, "Today I ate and I will eat again tomorrow."

Introduction

This is the simplest book we have ever written. It is about asking ourselves two questions: For what am I most grateful? For what am I least grateful? These questions help us identify moments of consolation and desolation. For centuries prayerful people have found direction for their day and for their life by identifying these moments.

I (Dennis) first discovered the power of these two questions twenty-five years ago, when I taught on the Rosebud Sioux Indian reservation. I had just moved into a housing project and I decided to risk something new: inviting guests for a meal. I invited eight of my students to dinner. Since the most common meal on the reservation is soup, I spent the morning boiling soup bones. Then I added a cupful of rice. It seemed to disappear. The same thing happened when I added the entire box of rice. Not knowing that rice expands as it cooks, I went to four different neighbors and collected about two more boxfuls of rice. (Unfortunately for me, Sioux are very generous and give without asking any questions . . .) With three boxes of rice in the kettle, I hoped I would have enough for eight hungry students if I first filled them up with plenty of bread. Questioning the wisdom of inviting so many people for dinner, I left the soup on the stove to simmer and headed over to school for class.

When I returned home with the students, the rice met us at the front door. The inside of my house looked as though a foot of snow had fallen. While some students stayed to help me shovel rice, others headed out to invite their families and friends to help us eat it. Instead of eight Sioux students, that night I fed most of the inhabitants of the reservation (dogs included). The meal made such a lasting impression that this past year when we gave a retreat on the same reservation, the most common question I heard was, "Dennis, you got any more rice soup?"

I remember the rice soup not just because it launched my cooking career, but also because it began a spiritual practice that is still fundamental to my life. That evening after dinner, not only my students but also some of their parents, younger brothers and sisters, and other teachers stayed. I was so moved by their presence that I forgot the format for the prayer service I had planned, and instead simply shared what I felt. Lighting a candle to help me get centered, I told the group I had not felt grateful for the

rice that met me at the door when I arrived home. But I was deeply grateful that people of every age were meeting in my home to feast (on rice!) and to pray. Others began to share their own moments of least gratitude and most gratitude from the day, each one lighting a candle as he or she spoke. God's will is generally for us to do more of whatever we are most grateful for or whatever gives us most life. That evening gave us all so much life that during the rest of my time on the reservation I cooked dinner every Friday (I stayed away from rice) and invited my Sioux students to come and eat, light a candle and share those two questions.

Today the three of us end most evenings sharing those same two questions. We have given retreats in over forty countries, and we find that regardless of culture or age group, these questions are the most helpful way for people to find direction for their lives. Twenty-five years later, the impact of the rice soup endures as every Sunday a group of faithful friends gathers in our home for dinner. We each light a candle and share our responses to those two questions. Which day we gather people—and the meal, thank God—have changed since I left the reservation, but the questions have not. We hope this book will help you to get as much life from them as we have.

Part I
The Examen

For many years, we have ended each day the same way. We light a candle, become aware of God's loving presence, and take about five minutes of quiet while we each ask ourselves two questions.

For what moment today am I most grateful?

For what moment today am I least grateful?

There are many other
ways to ask the same questions:

When did I give and receive
the most love today?
When did I give and receive
the least love today?

When did I feel most alive today?
When did I most feel life draining out of me?

When today did I have the greatest sense of belonging
to myself, others, God and the universe?
When did I have the least sense of belonging?

When was I happiest today?
When was I saddest?

What was today's high point?
What was today's low point?

Then we share these two moments with each other. Usually the entire process takes about twenty minutes. When we are very sleepy, we can easily finish in ten. We call this process the examen.

Several nights ago when we did this process together, here is what happened. For each of us, our moments of desolation had to do with the health of Matt and Dennis' father, Sheila's father-in-law. We had planned to take Matt and Dennis' father and mother on a Christmas holiday vacation at a cousin's home in Florida. We canceled the vacation because Dad had too much pain in his leg. That day he had told us he was thinking of selling the home he had lived in for fifty years. He asked us to pray for him to die. Our desolation that evening included grieving the lost holiday vacation and especially imagining what it would be like to live without our Dad or our home.

All three of us also mentioned the same consolation, a conversation we had earlier that day about the examen. It was triggered by a phone call from one family and a letter from another, telling us how much the examen had added to their lives. We realized how often the examen had given us life. Even now, in the midst of our desolation over Dad's health, the process of sharing these feelings with one another in the examen was giving us the strength to cope with the situation. Because the examen was giving us so much life, we decided that, since we would be at home rather than in Florida, we would spend the next week beginning this book. With all our books we have found that whatever we write about becomes more alive for us as we share it with others. So, we knew that the examen would become even more life-giving for us as we share it with you.

Why We Need the Examen

I (Matt) need the examen because of my pessimistic outlook. I am one of those who feels bad when he feels good for fear he will feel worse when he feels better. (In Africa I did manage to find a more pessimistic person. When I told him that we should change our pessimism because optimists live longer, he replied, "It serves them right!") I am also a perfectionist. At a workshop, ten people might compliment me while only one person might tell me something that could be improved. I forget the ten compliments and remember only what could be improved. I need the examen to help me notice not only what goes wrong but especially what goes right.

Each night I first get in touch with what I am grateful for from the day and I give thanks. Then I ask what I am not so grateful for. When I discover something I am not grateful for, I name it, feel it, and appreciate that I am not denying it and God is with me in it. Healing occurs to the degree I welcome all my feelings and let myself be loved in them. In this way I honestly acknowledge pain and I take in love. Then I can usually fall asleep with a grateful heart.

Whatever I sleep on enters my unconscious. For example, when I have lost something or don't know an answer to a problem, often I wake up the next morning with the solution. Why? Because whatever I am thinking about when falling asleep continues to be processed in my unconscious during the night. If I go to bed grateful and expect to awaken saying "thank you," the gratitude bathes my unconscious and I awaken more grateful. But if I go to bed resentful, I fill my unconscious with more resentment and awaken ready to strike back. Learning this has even changed my dreams. I no longer fall off cliffs headlong into paralysis or death but now bounce back with more life. The longer I sleep with a grateful heart, the more I heal my unconscious. So now when the alarm rings, I can say, "I think I need another hour of healing my unconscious," and fall back asleep without feeling guilty.

The examen is important to me (Dennis) because it has helped me appreciate all day long how the voice of God speaks through those moments for which I am not so grateful. I am an optimist, the opposite of Matt. I think that I live in the best of all possible worlds, and Matt is afraid I'm right. . . . Matt needs the examen to remind himself of what has gone right, so that he can be grateful. However, my addiction (which I call "Peace at Any Price") is to always be grateful and happy and to never rock the boat. Thus I need the examen to help me acknowledge feelings of sadness and pain and hear how God is speaking through them.

For example, one day I felt relieved after writing what I thought was a good letter. But when I reread it, I noticed feelings of sadness and exhaustion. I knew that when I would do the examen that evening, my letter would probably be what I was least grateful for. Years ago, before I first started doing the examen, I probably would have reread that letter and, not being in touch with what I was feeling, mailed it. Although the examen began as a reflective process that I did only in the evening, now it has become a habit and I find myself reflecting in a similar way throughout the day. Although I didn't know initially what my sadness was about, I knew enough not to mail the letter. Two days later, when I recognized how to rewrite the letter, the sadness immediately left. As I rewrote the letter, I discovered what God speaking through my sadness wanted to say to me: "Dare to rock the boat and stand up for yourself." If I had mailed the initial letter and not listened to my sadness—the moment I was least grateful for— I might have become stuck in my addiction and missed what God wanted to tell me. Eventually, Peace at Any Price might have led me to burnout, since the deepest part of me yearned to go in the opposite direction and dare to rock the boat. Burnout comes not primarily from doing too much, but from doing what we don't really want to do—so that one foot is moving forward and the other foot is trying to run away.

I (Sheila) need the examen because it helps me to be who I am and not who I think I should be. As a child, I was not encouraged to trust myself. I learned to feel ashamed of my needs and desires and to deny them in an effort to accommodate what others seemed to expect of me. The examen has helped me learn to trust my needs and desires, as I watch the pattern of what brings me consolation and desolation.

For example, several years ago when I was in school, Alex was one of my teachers. Alex was about my parents' age, and he was like a father to me. I was still fearful and withdrawn at that time, and Alex was the person I trusted most in the world. The relationship ended abruptly, for reasons I never fully understood. It took me many years to recover, and I always thought of this experience as the most painful one in my life. It was the only significant relationship I had ever had that seemed fundamentally broken. I tried several times to initiate a process of reconciliation, without success. I felt deeply ashamed of my inability to accept the situation as it was. I told myself repeatedly that some things do not heal in this life and I should stop bothering Alex with my desires for healing. However, such thoughts always brought great desolation in the form of an ache in my chest and a terrible sadness in my throat.

I noticed that even many years later I still needed to tell the story of this relationship and its traumatic ending over and over again to a few close friends. Each time I told it and felt heard, I felt consolation, as the ache in my chest and the sadness in my throat lifted somewhat. As I listened to my consolation, I realized that what I wanted most from Alex was for him to hear my experience of our relationship, even if it could not be restored. I needed to tell him why the rupture in our relationship had hurt me so badly and how much he meant to me. The ache in my chest and the lump in my throat were unexpressed pain and gratitude, relieved somewhat whenever I could share those feelings with another. The one I really needed to share them with was Alex. I wrote him a letter clarifying what I needed from him (to be heard) and what I did not need (a restoration of the father-daughter relationship we once had). To my surprise, he agreed to a meeting.

From the moment that I began to speak, I experienced Alex listening to me with profound care and attentiveness. He listened for three hours. As it turned out, he had not understood any more than I had the rupture in our relationship, and hearing the story was as healing for him as it was for me. By the time I finished, we both knew the barrier between us had dissolved and we were friends again.

Before I left, I told Alex that the time I had missed him most was when Dennis and I were married and he was not present to share in giving me away. When Dennis and I returned to see him again the next day, he gave us a gift-wrapped package containing a hand-made wedding gift. Yesterday we talked with Alex on the phone, as casually as if the intervening years of separation had never happened.

Because my mother was mentally ill and unable to connect with her children, I learned as a small child to feel ashamed of my needs and desires, especially needs for connectedness with other human beings. It was this voice of shame that told me I should give up on trying to heal my relationship with Alex. When I considered giving in to this voice, I felt desolation. When I got in touch with the consolation I felt each time I told the story of Alex, it showed me how to find healing: by asking to be heard.

The pattern I have described in myself, of feeling ashamed of my needs and desires, is an aspect of co-dependency. I behave like a co-dependent whenever I orient myself around the reality of others rather than living in my own reality and honoring my needs. Many people working in the field of addictions are saying that co-dependency and the core emotion of shame underlie all other addictions.

I need the examen to help me in my recovery. In her book, *Co-Dependence,* Anne Wilson Schaef says that for a recovering co-dependent, "even the smallest lie can plunge us back into our disease." In other words, distorting the truth of who I am in any way (to please others, to meet my expectations of who I *should* be or what I *should* feel) is like an alcoholic taking that first drink. I need the examen each day because it helps me get better at telling the truth about who I am and what I need.

The Examen Can Guide Our Lives

The examen makes us aware of moments that at first we might easily pass by as insignificant, moments that ultimately can give direction for our lives. For example, one day we were at an English/Spanish conference in the U.S. where the Anglos played music in the morning and the Hispanics played in the afternoon. That evening at examen, the moment all three of us were least grateful for was the same: the way the conference had dragged when the Anglos played. Our moment of most gratitude was also the same: the Hispanic group and how their music revived the conference.

At first glance, those two moments seemed insignificant. But during the next few months, we all noticed a pattern in which often our moments of gratitude centered around Hispanic people. If this had only happened a few times, we might have ignored it. But because we did the examen regularly and Hispanics were so often our experience of consolation, we realized we were in touch with something significant. We finally took time to ask ourselves what we should do about it. We knew that God's will for us is, whenever possible, to do more of whatever gives us the most life or gratitude. So, we decided to study Spanish in Bolivia and spend the following three years giving retreats in Latin America. Insignificant moments when looked at each day become significant because they form a pattern that often points the way to how God wants to give us more life.

When Other People Want Us To Tell Them What To Do

Many people who come to us bring questions such as, "Should I change jobs?" "Should I spend more time at home or in serving others?" "What can help me with my depression?" If we took responsibility for answering all these questions, we would exhaust ourselves and mislead others. However, the examen has given us a way of responding that protects us from pretending to be gurus who have all the answers and also protects the questioner from denying his or her own inner wisdom. We usually suggest that the person spend the next month focusing each day on what gave life and what drained life. Such people often return a month later having discovered from their own experience what they should do more of and what they should do less of in order to resolve their problem. The will of God is that we give and receive more love and life.

Everyday Experience Is Divine Revelation

St. Ignatius wrote *The Spiritual Exercises,* which have guided retreatants for centuries. The *Exercises* begin by recommending that everyone be taught the examen. Ignatius would not have been surprised that the examen revealed a direction for our life, since the examen is what changed him from a wild soldier to a pilgrim walking barefoot to Jerusalem. He expected that God would speak through our deepest feelings and yearnings, what he called "consolation" and "desolation." For us, consolation is whatever helps us connect with ourselves, others, God and the universe. Desolation is whatever disconnects us. Ignatius recommended returning to our deepest moments of consolation and desolation. We do this because,

> It is wisely said, "Experience is the best teacher."... The primary and most obvious reason for this is that revelation is not over, God is constantly revealing himself to us in our experience.... Of course, the Bible is divine revelation—no one denies that. *But so is life!* It is precisely because God is present to life and available to human experience that *we* have a divinely inspired story to tell, and that the story once told is revelation.

One reason we light a candle when we do the examen is because the candle's flame symbolizes the light of divine revelation in our everyday experience. The gratitude questions we use are simply one way of discovering the day's consolation and desolation, the interior movements through which divine revelation unfolds. Ignatius saw the examen as the cornerstone of spiritual life to the extent that when the Jesuits at the Council of Trent asked if they could skip their prayer exercises because they had no time, Ignatius told them to skip anything but the examen.

Finding Our Sealed Orders

As we do this examen process every day, a pattern emerges that is even deeper than the pattern that leads to a specific decision such as our commitment to study Spanish in Bolivia. Agnes Sanford referred to this pattern as our "sealed orders" from God. By this she meant that it is as if,

before we were born, each of us talked over with God the special purpose of our time on earth. Throughout our lives each of us discovers more and more deeply our unique sealed orders, a way that only we are gifted to give and receive love.

When I (Sheila) am in touch with the special purpose of my life and carrying out my sealed orders, I have a profound feeling of consolation or rightness and my whole body relaxes. I believe this sense of rightness expresses itself physiologically because the purpose of our life is built into the very cells of our body.

I have noticed this sense of rightness whenever I am in touch with or learning about the inner goodness of created things. Looking back, I realize that this has guided all my major decisions in life. I became a Christian (my family is Jewish) because I sensed the presence of Jesus in nature. I went to seminary (instead of a graduate program in psychology) because I wanted to learn about the presence of God in human development. In seminary I took every course on science and theology and ultimately became a Roman Catholic because of Catholicism's profound incarnational sense—its recognition of the presence of God in all things. I married Dennis because he shares my joy in finding this goodness in creation.

Because the purpose of our lives is built into every cell of our bodies, we don't need to look far to find it. We can find it by looking near, in the little everyday things that give us consolation and desolation. I experience consolation when I see the leaves of a plant turned toward the sun, when I sense the vitality in whole foods as I prepare them, or when I feel the life energy in natural cotton clothing. Many such moments have suggested to me that my sealed orders are to recognize the face of God in all things and to help each thing become more truly itself by my loving presence to it.

Moments of desolation are equally instructive. Recently we gave a retreat at which we spoke about the presence of God in evolution. A few of the participants objected strenuously and with considerable hostility, insisting that evolution is "against the Bible." I felt great sadness and at a loss as to how to communicate with these people. I have learned from this and similar experiences that I am not gifted to work with people with whom I cannot share my love for the created world.

Robert Johnson suggests that we summarize the special purpose of our life in a single word or phrase that "names" who we are. Once we know who we are, we also know who we are not. We know where and with whom we belong, and we can cease trying to be all things to all people. As I have reflected on the pattern of consolation and desolation in my life, the name that fits my experience is "cherishing every creature's inner goodness."

Sharing the Examen with Another

Although the examen is helpful when done alone, we do it together. When we share with another, not only do the moments we choose to speak about become more real and important to us, but so do the people with whom we share. This is why Twelve Step groups (the fastest-growing spirituality in the United States) put so much emphasis on regular sharing with another, e.g., a sponsor. In fact, Steps Four, Five and Ten, which invite us to review our lives and share the results with another, are a variation on the examen. In a sense, most Twelve Step meetings are group examens in which participants share their consolation and desolation since the previous meeting. This sharing facilitates bonding as it deepens group members' empathy and compassion for one another. In such an environment, people can heal, grow and work together. We have noticed this at other kinds of meetings as well. If participants begin the meeting by sharing the consolation and desolation they bring with them, they can usually complete the tasks of the meeting in half the time because they are bonded and better able to listen.

In our case, sharing the examen gives us a chance to enter into one another's hearts. We are surprised by how often what for one of us is the moment of most gratitude, is for another the moment for which he or she is least grateful. For instance, my (Dennis') favorite country is Guatemala. My favorite recreation there is bartering in artisan markets where everything is handmade with beautiful, rainbow colors. One evening, during a trip to Guatemala, I shared with Sheila and Matt that I was most grateful for being able to buy six handwoven shirts. Because I had bartered the price per shirt from $12 down to $4, I had bought one for myself and five for my friends. That same evening Sheila reported my bartering as her moment of least gratitude. Sheila makes things by hand (she knitted sweaters for everyone in our family), and she knew that each shirt would take about five days to make. So when the seller said, "$12," rather than me offering $4, Sheila wanted me to say "$24." We returned to Guatemala again last year. This time, before I bartered in the market, I bartered with Sheila about what would be a fair price. At the end of that day when we did the examen, we all agreed that our moment of most gratitude was the shirt purchase we made in which both the seller and ourselves felt like winners.

Sharing the Examen as a Family

One of our greatest joys in teaching the examen process at retreats has been the number of families who have taken it home and made it a regular part of their lives together. For example, Frank has passed on the examen to his five children and ten grandchildren. Four years ago Frank was visiting three-year-old Martha, six-year-old Eric and their parents. The adults began talking about how their day went, and Frank thought to tell them about the examen process. The children caught on immediately. They began asking each other, "What was your best part of the day?" and "What was your worst part of the day?"

Four years later, this family is still doing the examen together. The examen has given them an opportunity for reconciliation and making amends to one another. For example, one evening Eric's desolation was the time during the day when he was mean to someone and had to take a "time out." Another time Eric shared that his best part of the day was when he squirted the hose all over Martha and soaked her. Martha said her worst part of the day was getting drenched. At that point their father intervened and gently guided both children in reconciling with each other. Eric and Martha are learning from the examen that one person's best part of the day might be another's worst part of the day, and to respect each other in their differences.

Another example is Jim, Ann and their three children. They have been doing the examen consistently every evening since we taught it to them eleven years ago. Sometimes the whole family gathers around the table and does the examen together. Other times, Jim or Ann does it with each of the children while putting that child to bed. They have adapted the questions as follows:

What did you feel good about today?

What was your biggest struggle today, or when did you feel sad, helpless or angry?

After sharing his or her answers, each person then brings them to God in thanksgiving for the consolation and in prayers for help with the desolation.

When we asked Jim about the results of having done this process together for so many years, he said,

> The examen has taught my children to trust themselves. They know that God is in all of reality, not only out there but in the core of life and in themselves. Last night our fifteen-year-old daughter Beth turned down an invitation to her first date with a very popular and handsome boy who wanted to take her to a party where there would be a lot of drinking and sexually promiscuous behavior. She knew she didn't want to be in that kind of environment. The boy was so impressed with her sense of herself that he left the party early and came over to visit with Beth at our home. They talked for a while and he returned to the party with the intention of being the designated driver for anyone who had too much to drink. I think Beth's inner strength has come from all these years of doing the examen and learning to trust that she knows what gives her life and what doesn't.
>
> Beth shared this whole experience with us, just as she shares everything significant in her life. The other children are equally transparent and open. For example, nine-year-old Tom's older friend, Bert, is dying of Alzheimer's. During examen recently, Tom's desolation was "I don't understand why Bert is losing his mind and dying such a terrible death." This began a long conversation in which Tom, only nine years old, faced an ultimate issue like death. His older brother, thirteen-year-old Sam, is in the midst of puberty and quite overwhelmed by his sexual feelings. But he shares them with us, rather than saving them for the locker room as most children his age would do.
>
> I think the examen protects our children not only from drinking and premature sexuality, but also from getting caught up in the violence of our culture. Many of their peers try to resolve conflicts by beating each other up or bringing guns and knives to school. But the examen has taught our children to face the violence in their own shadow sides and bring it into the light for healing. So, they are can usually respond nonviolently to their friends and to larger issues of social justice.
>
> My wife and I both work, and for our family as a whole, the examen has been a way of remaining connected despite our busy lives. It holds our family together and gives us a way of being emotionally present to one another.

In the midst of this conversation, Jim left the phone to check on Sam and Tom. When he returned, he told us that Sam had put his younger brother to bed and now both children were sleeping. He added, "I'm sure Sam did the examen with Tom before putting him to bed, because that's how our children have learned to go to sleep."

For Frank's family and Jim and Ann's family, sharing the examen is like giving one another the bread of life. In fact, another family we know does just that. They gather around the table in the evening with some bread. Each person breaks off a piece of the bread and holds it as he or she shares consolation and desolation from the day. Then they give their bread of life to one another.

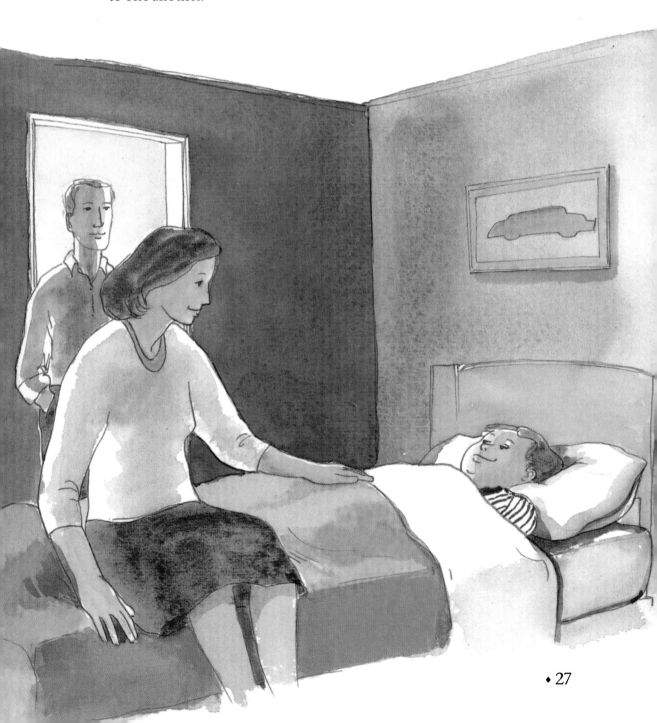

What If You Have No One To Share With?

What matters most in doing the examen is to experience an environment of unconditional love in which you feel safe to own your experience and feel all your feelings. This is one reason we encourage doing the examen with other people who love you.

How can you create this environment if you are alone? Some people may wish to return in their imagination to a memory of when they felt the most sense of belonging to themselves, others, God or the universe. Others may find it helpful to imagine a trusted friend, Jesus, or God as they understand God sitting beside them. Still others may wish to imagine themselves in a peaceful natural setting where they feel connected to the earth, such as by a stream. Another way that helps may be to play some favorite music. For some people it is helpful to do all of these. What matters most is not who or what you imagine, but that you find a way that evokes for you a felt sense of the unconditional love of God. This can be even more effective if you take a moment to consciously breathe in that unconditional love and let it fill you again.

At the point of sharing your experience, if you have no one else physically present with whom to verbalize your consolation and desolation, you may find it helpful to express yourself in some other way. For some it may be journaling, for others drawing or movement, or any other way of expressing your experience.

Examen Process

Preparation: You may wish to light a candle. Do whatever helps you to experience unconditional love. For example, imagine yourself in a favorite place with someone whose love you trust, such as a friend, Jesus or God as you understand God. Put your feet flat on the floor, take a few deep breaths from the bottom of your toes, up through your legs, your abdominal muscles and your chest. Breathe in that unconditional love, and when you breathe out, fill the space around you with it.

1. Place your hand on your heart and ask Jesus or God as you understand God to bring to your heart the moment today for which you are *most grateful.* If you could relive one moment, which one would it be? When were you most able to give and receive love today?

Ask yourself what was said and done in that moment that made it so special. Breathe in the gratitude you felt and receive life again from that moment.

2. Ask God to bring to your heart the moment today for which you are *least grateful.* When were you least able to give and receive love?

Ask yourself what was said and done in that moment that made it so difficult. Be with whatever you feel without trying to change or fix it in any way. You may wish to take deep breaths and let God's love fill you just as you are.

3. *Give thanks* for whatever you have experienced. If possible, share as much as you wish of these two moments with a friend.

Part II
Nine Hundred Candles

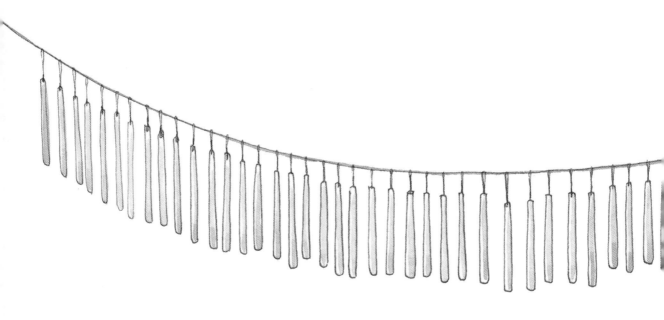

In the Guatemalan mountain village of Chichicastenango, a candle vendor has a tiny shop about the size of a phone booth. It is so small that the only place available for his wares is the ceiling, from which hang hundreds of candles. On a good day, he may sell thirty or even forty candles.

Several years ago we bought ten candles from him. After we returned to the United States, we discovered something wonderful about his candles. They don't drip. For years previously, we had gatherings in which people would light candles and share their responses to the examen questions. And for years, no matter how careful people were, we had to clean up candle wax after they left.

So on our next trip to Guatemala, we made a special trip to the candle shop in Chichicastenango. With as straight a face as possible, we nonchalantly asked for nine hundred candles. The vendor, probably thinking that we were having trouble with Spanish, happily counted out nine candles and handed them to us. When we repeated our request, he added ten more thinking we meant "nineteen." When he finally understood that we meant what we said, he declared, "Que milagro!" ("What a miracle!")

Thus far we have shared how to use the examen to put us in touch with our consolation and desolation at the end of each day. This section will include some of the other ways we have used those nine hundred candles. Let us know if you want directions to the shop in Chichicastenango. Could you bring us back nine hundred more candles?

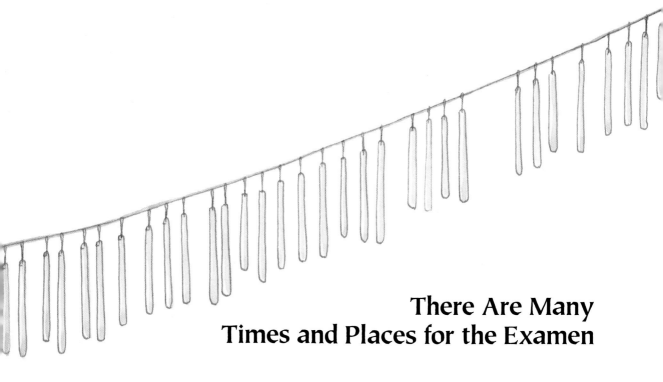

There Are Many
Times and Places for the Examen

We do the examen questions as a way of reflecting upon any signifi-cant experience or period of time. We do it over a part of a day, following

a conversation

a meeting

a class

a movie

a meal (consolation for us if it was Chinese . . .)

We stop in the midst of a project when we feel stuck, or in a discussion that is turning into an argument.

We do the examen over an entire day.

We do the examen over our week, by asking ourselves, "What am I most grateful for during the past week? What am I least grateful for?" Dennis and Sheila do this each week with a group that gathers in their home every Sunday afternoon, followed by dinner. Matt does this every Thursday morning (at 7:30 AM!) with five members of his Jesuit community.

Often on special occasions we invite friends to share the examen. For example, on New Year's Day we all share when we gave and received the most and least love during the past year. On St. Patrick's Day we share what we are most and least grateful for in our Irish (or Jewish, Vietnamese, African, etc.) heritage. On the Fourth of July, we share how our country has given us life and how it has taken life from us during the past year. On the anniversary of a loved one's death or on Memorial Day, we share when we felt the most consolation and the most desolation in the grieving process.

There are many places where we might want to do the examen, and people with whom we can do it. For many of us, the most natural setting for the examen is with a close friend or a spouse, with whom we already share our lives. If we attend a support group, this may be another place where we can do the examen as a way of sharing ourselves with the group. Those who meet regularly with a spiritual companion, confessor or therapist may want to include the examen as a way of sharing their process of growth. Teachers may want to do the examen with their students, and supervisors with their employees. (Students may want to do it with their teachers, and employees with their supervisors, too!)

Doing Only the First Examen Question

There are no rules about doing the examen, and at any of the times we have suggested (daily, weekly, yearly, Fourth of July, St. Patrick's Day, etc.) we may focus only on the positive side of the question if we wish. For example, we used to find writing Christmas greetings a draining experience, but for the past five years we have found ourselves looking forward to it.

The change came when we started adding one or two sentences telling the person why we are especially grateful for him or her. We now enjoy this so much that we send over five hundred letters each year. This has not only become our way of giving thanks to those who touch our lives but also a way for us to remember the moments during the past year for which we are especially grateful. Thus by the time Christmas approaches we find ourselves filled with gratitude. We try to do this not just with Christmas greetings but every time we write a thank-you note or send a card.

Writing cards is just one of the times when it may be more appropriate to do only the first examen question, "What am I most grateful for?" rather than going on to include our moment of least gratitude. For example, on birthdays, anniversaries or Valentine's Day, we may wish to tell people we love what we have appreciated most about them during the past year.

One family we know does this every New Year's. While their children were small, they gathered together and each took a turn telling all the other family members what he or she most appreciated about each one during the past year. Since the children have moved away, they now continue this practice by letter. Every New Year's, each family member writes a letter to each of the others, sharing gratitude for that person during the past year.

We need not wait for special events to do this. For example, many of us are accustomed to blessing the food when we gather together for a meal. Often "grace" means a perfunctory formula we use to thank God for the food. But some families take a moment of quiet and allow each person to get in touch with what he or she really is grateful for and share it with the group. In other families, the person designated to "say grace" expresses how he or she is especially grateful for each person present or for whatever has happened in the life of the family that day.

Besides families, the positive examen can help create a loving environment in many other situations. For example, our friend Susan struggled with discipline problems in her fourth-grade classroom. Then, on Mondays she began asking each child to draw the name of another student and to observe him or her throughout the rest of the week. On Fridays each child reported to the entire class all the good things noticed about the classmate whose name he or she had drawn. As these children used the positive examen to create a classroom environment in which everyone felt valued and appreciated, their discipline problems disappeared. Like these fourth-graders, we are all longing for someone to help us discover our goodness.

Examen of the Past Year

For about twenty years Matt and I (Dennis) met with a group of six Jesuits each summer at a lake. Each person took half a day to share his year and hear the other's reactions. We did this because we wanted to be known by one another so well that we could help each other discern new directions. For example, several times Matt and I shared how giving occasional retreats brought us the most life. After hearing this for several years, the group suggested we spend less time in our jobs (Matt was teaching the Sioux and I was the superior of a Jesuit community) in order to do more part time retreat work. When we shared their discernment with our provincial, he told us to take the next fifteen years to do retreat work not just part time, but full time. Our Jesuit group launched us into a ministry that, almost twenty years later, we still do together.

When Sheila and I married, we decided to invite some friends who knew both of us to meet with us annually so that we could continue to experience together what I had experienced the past twenty years. Although meeting with this group means that we drive more than one thousand miles, we just returned from our sixth annual meeting. This was at least the twenty-sixth time that I have annually reviewed my life with friends, yet I was surprised once again. Just before this meeting, our eleventh book, *Good Goats: Healing Our Image of God* was published. This book says that God loves us at least as much as the person who loves us the most, which means that God never vengefully punishes us. We wrote *Good Goats* to help people change their image of God from a vengeful punisher to an unconditional lover because we've found that we copy the characteristics not just of our parents but also of the God we adore. What became clear for me as I shared with our friends the consolation of publishing *Good Goats* was that I now felt as if I had completed my life's work. I heard myself saying that if I never did anything else with my life, it would feel complete. My life's work seems to be giving God a good reputation (and healing the ways I and others have been frightened and shamed by religious teaching that gives God a bad reputation).

When I shared my desolation from the year, it was the amount of time Sheila and I spent getting our Colorado home ready for rental during ski season. The contrast between our consolation and desolation helped us realize once again that our ministry is writing and giving retreats with Matt, and not the house rental business. When we returned home we decided that we would stop renting out our home to strangers, even though this means a substantial reduction in our income. We already look forward to next year's one-thousand-mile drive to see what surprises we'll find as I do my twenty-seventh annual sharing with friends.

Healing the Future

Ann's voice on the phone was frantic:

The doctors say my liver cancer is back and there's nothing more they can do. The whole family is wound up tight and nearly crazy. Can you come and help us?

When I (Matt) arrived at Ann's home, fear electrified the air. So I asked each family member a question: What do you fear the most (or are least grateful for) as you face the future of Ann's imminent death? Ann said, "I fear leaving Al all alone after forty years of a happy marriage. Who will take care of him if he has one of his choking spells at night?" Al said, "I'm not worried about my choking but I worry about how the time we still have can be the best days of Ann's life. And I fear trying to live without Ann at my side. We shared everything, even my business decisions." Their daughter, Teresa, said, "Mom, I was counting on you to be a grandmother for Michael. I'm afraid I won't know how to be as good a mother for my son as you were for me." In naming their fears of the future, this family was naming and getting in touch with what meant the most to them: the loving presence of each other. Their faces that had been frozen in fear were now flowing with tears of appreciation and compassionate love. Sharing their fears had brought them closer together than ever.

So I asked the second question: "What is helping you now (what are you most grateful for) as you face all this?" Ann spoke of breaking into tears in the department store when she overheard another Christmas shopper say that she would buy a new coat next year rather than this year. "I don't have a next year to dream about. But that also means I won't need a new coat. I won't need the coats and other things I already have. So I've been giving my things away to special people and telling them why. Sharing my things gives me so much joy."

Her daughter-in-law spoke up, "It's like this necklace you gave me. I felt so close to you when you said my husband gave you two special gifts: this necklace that took all his savings at age eight and then fourteen years later his bringing me into your family in marriage. Knowing you trust me with your son helps me face my fears of the future. I think I can help Teresa be a mother to Michael."

Others named special moments when they had cried together, prayed together and laughed together (like the time Ann threw her gum right at a bald head two pews ahead in church). They realized they had the resources they needed as a family to face the future.

Healing the future happens whenever we can ask the two examen questions about what gives and takes life. What do I fear will take life in the future? What gives (or, in the future, could give) me life as I face this? When I know my needs and the resources available to me, the future loses its power to terrify me. When I left Ann's home that night, even two-year-old Michael knew that although he was losing his grandmother he would have all the love he needed.

Final Examen

Sometime or other, most of us ask ourselves, "Is this all there is to life? What can I do to feel alive again? Should I change jobs, go to school, or what?" These questions are all ways of asking whether we are carrying out the purpose of our life. The purpose of our life often preoccupies us at times of transition and crisis, such as career changes or the transition from young adulthood to midlife. In fact, the question of whether we are really carrying out the purpose of our life is usually the root of what is commonly called the "midlife crisis." Earlier in this book, we spoke of how the examen can help us discover our sealed orders, the special purpose of our life. The final examen is another way of getting in touch with our sealed orders.

For example, for the twenty years that I (Matt) had known him, Sam struggled with chronic worry and overwork. He always looked exhausted. The last time I saw him, after four years apart, I knew from the peace on Sam's face that something within him had changed for the better. Two years earlier, Sam had gone on a retreat, during which the person guiding him made the following suggestion:

> In your prayer imagine that you are seventy-five years old and dying. See the events of your life flash before you. For what are you grateful? What do you wish you had done differently? Pay special attention to the years between your present age and your death.

When I commented on the change I saw in him, Sam said,

> After that exercise of a final examen of my life, I knew I didn't want to die in front of a computer screen. I wished I had spent the remainder of my life counseling alcoholics and broken families. So I quit my computer job and began taking college classes to get a counseling degree. Meanwhile I've been working as a lay counselor with alcoholics. Since that decision I enjoy life, and I feel at peace that I'm doing what I was sent here to do.

After seeing the change in Sam, I decided to do the final examen myself. As I reviewed my life, I was grateful for all I was now doing: writing, giving retreats, training spiritual directors, and being superior of my Jesuit community. But even here I saw priorities. For example, I was most grateful for

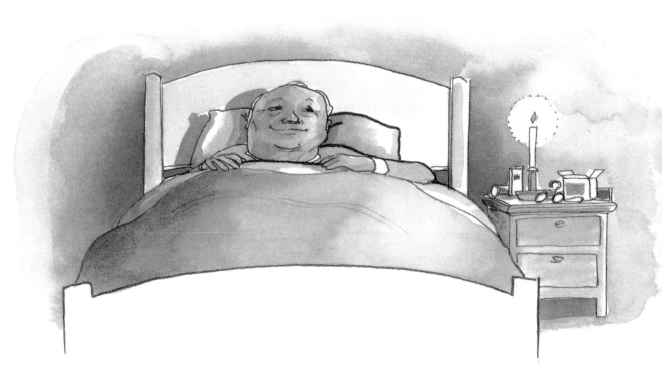

the writing that encourages me to be reflective now and will endure after my death. I was least grateful for being a superior. I don't want to die at seventy-five being a superior! Since doing that final examen, although writing is the most difficult thing I do, I have made it a greater priority. Before this, it took us five years to write *Belonging: Bonds of Healing & Recovery*. Since then, we have written three more books (including this one) in just two years.

Fishing and gardening with my dad have also become a priority, since I realized during the final examen how much I want to spend time with my parents while they are still alive. When I told my father about the final examen, he said, "It won't work for me. I am already eighty-three." So I told him to try being ninety-five and on his deathbed. It worked, and he too decided fishing and gardening with me were a priority.

So, to live the rest of your life fully and to enjoy it more, you might want to imagine you are seventy-five and dying. For what are you grateful? For what are you least grateful and wish you had done differently with your life?

Giving Our Bread Away

This book began with the image of World War II orphan children sleeping with bread to reassure them that they would eat tomorrow as they did today. Many of them survived the concentration camps only because other prisoners had given their own last piece of bread to these children. Viktor Frankl wrote of how this bread brought not just survival but also hope and interior freedom:

> We who lived in concentration camps can remember the men who walked through the huts comforting others, giving away their last piece of bread. They may have been few in number . . . but they offer sufficient proof that everything can be taken from a man but one thing: the last of his freedoms—to choose one's attitude in any given set of circumstances, to choose one's own way.

When we sleep with bread we are empowered to choose our own way under any circumstances. We become like the men and women in the concentration camps who could give others the bread of life they held.

Part III
Questions & Answers

Do you have questions about the examen process? Following are the questions others have most often asked us.

Will this examen process keep me from making mistakes and wrong decisions?

The examen does have some safeguards built into it that can help us avoid mistakes and wrong decisions. For example, it gives us a process for reflecting upon our choices over time, rather than acting hastily. Before making an important decision, we can watch for a pattern of consolation and desolation over many weeks, months or perhaps even years.

However, as long as we are human nothing can guarantee that we will never make a mistake or a wrong decision. What the examen does do is allow mistakes and wrong decisions to become opportunities for learning and growth.

For example, what I (Matt) was most grateful for Sunday night was my decision to stay home the following day from my aunt's wake. I felt consolation, relieved that I would not have to make the three-hour trip. I thought I could make better use of that time preparing her funeral liturgy for Tuesday. But the following night (Monday) my desolation was that I had stayed home from her wake and missed the opportunity to visit with family members. How could I have made such a mistake that resulted in my consolation of one night leading to my desolation of the next night?

I think it was because Sunday night I was very tired and I only asked myself the first examen question, "What was I most grateful for today?" I did not ask the second question "What was I not so grateful for today?" If I had, I would have felt the grief and fear growing inside me that in losing the last of my Linn aunts, I was now going to lose my relationship with her entire side of the family. I would then have realized that my need to connect with my relatives was greater than my need to prepare the perfect funeral liturgy. This experience taught me that I can avoid making some mistakes by asking both examen questions instead of just one.

The examen can improve our odds of avoiding mistakes and wrong decisions, and when we do make mistakes it can help us catch them sooner rather than later. But perhaps its greatest gift is that it can help us turn mistakes and wrong decisions into opportunities to learn and grow.

You are encouraging me to be with and listen to desolation as well as consolation. I was taught to resist or go against desolation. Why are you saying the opposite?

We agree that our attitude toward desolation is somewhat different than you may have been taught. Our present attitude is somewhat different from what *we* were taught, too. We were taught that many of our desolations, such as feelings of lust, anger, etc., were sinful. Sometimes such feeling states were called "capital sins." The truth in this teaching is that we need to resist the impulse to act upon feelings in a way that would be harmful to ourselves or others. For example, feelings of lust if acted upon might result in promiscuity, or feelings of anger if acted upon might result in violence.

Yet this teaching often missed the distinction between acting upon feelings and listening to their story. Such teaching assumed that if we resisted certain feelings, they would go away. However, this isn't how our feelings work. When feelings are ignored or resisted, they grow inside us and are likely to eventually lead to an explosion in which we act out in even more destructive ways than we might have at first. We believe that what negative feelings or desolations really want is not destructive behavior but rather to have their story heard. When their story is heard, they are satisfied and they quiet down naturally. If we then take steps to meet the needs revealed by the story, this desolation is unlikely to recur.

Our emphasis on hearing the story behind our desolation is consistent with the teaching of great spiritual writers like St. Ignatius. When, for example, we follow his suggestion to look at the beginning, middle and end of any temptation or his suggestion to discover the roots of what he called "sin," we are beginning to listen to the story of our desolation. Any process can help reveal the story of our desolation if it puts us in touch with what started it (the beginning), what keeps it going now (the middle) and what it needs to be resolved (the end). Contemporary psychology, which has helped us understand the nature of the unconscious, the dynamics of emotions and the results of emotional wounding, has given us new tools for hearing our desolation's story. Sheila will describe more fully later (pages 52-54) how she used one of these tools to hear the story of her desolation regarding her relationship with Alex. Although Ignatius intuited the need to listen to the story of our desolation, many of these tools were unavailable to him.

What if I don't want to be with my desolation, or feel afraid to hear its story?

Since what ultimately heals is love, we can begin by letting ourselves be loved in the midst of our resistance and fear. The most important thing is not that we understand our desolation, but rather that we let ourselves be loved. Sometimes we do not let ourselves be in touch with the story of our desolation because it is too painful or threatening, and we don't feel safe enough to face it. Then we may need to set aside for a while our effort to figure it out and just take in love. For example, we may need to share many times with a friend before we will feel safe enough, and then the story of our desolation may reveal itself to us.

We are naturally meant to be in touch with the story of our experience. However, many of us have learned to repress or deny what our desolation wants to say to us, through family background and through our culture that teaches us to avoid and deny pain. The examen is a way of relearning this skill, and if we do it each day we probably will get better at hearing what our desolation is trying to say to us. So, just by doing the examen over time, the capacity to consciously know what our desolation wants to say will grow.

What if I don't know what my desolation is trying to say to me?

Often what your desolation most wants to say to you is, "I need you to do more of what consistently brings you the most consolation." Thus, the answer to what your desolation is trying to say may be found right within your consolation. What we feel grateful for in a day is generally something that has an energy we need, and what we feel not so grateful for generally involves a frustrated or unmet need. Thus, our consolation may reveal to us (and help meet) the unmet need behind our desolation.

For example, we have shared that over a period of many months we discovered a pattern of consolation whenever we interacted with Hispanic people. In order to do more of what was bringing us consolation, we decided to study Spanish in Bolivia and spend three years giving retreats in Latin America.

It is only now that I (Dennis) know why it was important for me to go to Latin America. For years a desolation for me was my inability to express on the outside what I was feeling on the inside. A symptom of this was that even though I always loved music, I could never express rhythmically with my body what was inside my heart. I knew that I would be healed to the extent that I learned to dance. During our years in Latin America, I realized that the gift of Hispanic people is to express on the outside what they are feeling on the inside. In a sense they are always dancing, and they taught me how. When I came home from Latin America, for the first time in my life I could move rhythmically.

When I decided to follow my consolation and go to Latin America, I had no idea how this would give my desolation what it most needed: the ability to dance. I learned that whenever I do more of what consistently gives me the most consolation, I can be confident that I am hearing an important part of what my desolation wants to say to me.

When I (Matt) don't know what my desolation is saying, I sometimes find it helpful to change the examen question. For example, I often notice at the end of a day that my desolation occurred during moments when I was pessimistic and negative. When I want to explore this pattern, I change the examen questions to:

> What helped me most with my pessimism and negativity today?
> What helped me least with my pessimism and negativity today?

When I did this last week, I realized that four times I became pessimistic and negative when I was doing something because I *should* rather than because I *enjoyed* it. For example, I biked to the library just to enjoy the ride. On the way back I began thinking, "I should go faster because I spent too much time at the library." Immediately my peaceful, relaxed state changed to edginess and I began criticizing the holes in the road, the inconsiderate drivers and the unmowed grass. When I went back to just enjoying the ride, I felt peaceful again. This peace remained even through a difficult meeting that evening.

Last week I also learned how this "should" pattern is especially likely to trigger my negativity when I have to wait. For example, one day I was waiting in the check-out line at the grocery store. I felt angry at a woman (who had a million coupons she wanted to redeem) because I thought she stepped ahead of me. (Actually, she didn't.) I began speaking to myself negatively, saying things like, "You are wasting time because you stupidly picked the longest line again." There was a "should" underneath this: "You should get through this line faster so you can get home and enjoy yourself." Even trying to enjoy myself can get me trapped in shoulds. When

I told my Thursday morning sharing group about this, they all laughed, and so did I. Now I'll bet I can laugh at myself the next time I am waiting in the longest line.

I also learned that what helped me most with my pessimism and negativity last week was whenever I asked for or took time for what I needed. For example, on three afternoons, instead of forcing myself to continue writing, I decided I needed to take a break and swim. Another time I said to Dennis, "I need to talk to you about what you just said because it was hurtful to me." When I take time to ask for and care for my needs, then I don't get so negative at others because they haven't guessed my needs or met my unspoken expectations. But for me, it is difficult to ask for what I need. This, too, is rooted in a should that I learned in childhood: "You should be a loving person who sets aside his needs to care for others."

As the story of last week's negativity unfolds, I see other ways to change the examen questions this week:

When today did I ask for what I needed?
When today did I not ask for what I needed?

or

When today did I do something because I enjoyed it rather than because I should?
When today did I do something because I should rather than because I enjoyed it?

Thus, looking at the pattern of my pessimism and negativity over a week, I heard its story: what leads me into it, what keeps me in it and what resolves it. So, this week I should do more swimming, sharing, asking for my needs, and canceling all shoulds like this sentence. I should change next week's examen question to, "What am I doing because I should rather than because I enjoy it?" I should do that.

Is there anything else that especially helps you listen to your desolation?

The most useful tool for us is a prayer process called focusing, which helps us listen through our bodies. Even when we don't consciously know the story of our desolation, our bodies do know, since our bodies carry the meaning of all our experience. For example, I (Sheila) used focusing to help me listen to my desolation (and my consolation) in the story of my relationship with Alex.

The first step in this process is to get in touch with a part of yourself that needs to be listened to and cared for, as I did with the desolation I felt whenever I thought of giving up on trying to heal that relationship. Then ask yourself if you *want* to be with and listen to this part of yourself right now. If the answer is no, then just be with that no, without trying to fix or change it. The point is never to force yourself to do anything, but instead to care for yourself exactly as you are. If the answer is yes, the next step is to create a loving atmosphere where this part of you will feel safe to speak, just as you would prepare your home for a beloved friend or open your arms to a hurting child or a pet.

Once you have created a safe inner atmosphere, then become aware of how you are carrying this whole issue in your body. As I do this, the issue begins to speak to me through a word, an image, a memory or another bodily feeling. As I became aware of how I was carrying my relationship with Alex in my body, I felt an ache in my chest and a lump in my throat. As I let myself down into these feelings, they changed to a sense that I was choking on something stuck inside me. As I stayed with that, the words that came were, "I am choking on pain and on gratitude. I have to tell Alex how much he hurt me and I have to thank him for all he gave to me." As I recalled moments when I had shared these feelings with others and imagined sharing them with Alex, my chest and throat eased and the desolation changed to consolation. My body knew what my desolation was trying to say, even when my conscious mind did not.

We learned focusing and adapted it from the work of Peter Campbell and Edwin McMahon, who in turn learned and adapted it from Eugene Gendlin. If you would like to use this process yourself, the steps are as follows:

Focusing Prayer Process

1. Sit comfortably with your eyes closed. Let your awareness move down into the center of your body and notice what you feel there.

2. Get in touch with an experience of desolation (or of consolation).

3. Ask yourself if you *want* to listen to this part of yourself right now. Is it okay to spend some time with it? If not, care for the feeling of not wanting to spend time with this right now.

4. If it is okay to spend some time with this area of your life, take a few moments to create a loving atmosphere where it will feel safe to speak to you. For example, how would you prepare your home if your best friend were coming to visit? How would you reach out to a hurting child or a wounded pet?

5. Now let yourself down into how this whole thing feels inside you. Where in your body do you especially experience it? Perhaps you feel an ache in your chest, a lump in your throat, a knot in your stomach, shaking in your legs, etc.

6. Care for this feeling and see if it wants to tell you about itself, perhaps through a word, an image or a symbol. Perhaps it wants to come to you as a little child. Perhaps it wants to tell you its name, its history (when and how it developed) and what it needs.

7. Whatever comes, reach out to care for it without trying to change it or fix it. Or, maybe just put your hand on that part of your body in a caring way. If you wish, ask Jesus, God as you understand God, or some other trusted person to come and help you care for it.

8. Tell this part of you that you will come back at another time and listen to it some more.

9. Before concluding, notice how your body feels compared to when you began. Are you now carrying this issue differently in your body?

What if the same desolation recurs day after day?

Recurring daily situations of desolation may be putting us in touch with an underlying and unresolved hurt that is using those daily situations to keep trying to get our attention. It may be helpful to ask ourselves, "When in the past did I feel this the most?" For example, perhaps every time we hear about a death or go to a funeral we feel intense desolation. If we ask ourselves "When in the past did I feel this the most?" we may recall our own mother's death many years earlier for which we have not fully grieved.

Even minor desolations can put us in touch with deep underlying hurts. For example, I (Matt) have mentioned that often my desolation is moments when I was pessimistic and negative. I am especially likely to be this way when I have to wait in line. Last week when I was stuck in a long grocery check-out line, I asked myself when in the past I had felt this way the most. I thought of all the times as a child I waited in line to be chosen for teams at sports events. Because I was always the shortest boy, I was the last one chosen. I felt angry and helpless at being last. Thus, last week when I had to wait in line at the grocery store, I again felt helpless and angry that I would be last.

Most of our other books include ways to pray for healing of such painful memories (see Resources for Further Growth). In some cases, a recurring desolation may be an encouragement to get outside help, such as psychotherapy. We may also want to join a support group where we are sharing with people who are struggling with a similar desolation and who can encourage us as we seek healing.

You've explained why I should listen to my desolation, but I'm not so sure I should listen to my consolation. Can't following my consolation get me into trouble? For example, what if I feel consolation when I smoke a cigarette, over-work, drink with my friends or relate sexually to an inappropriate person?

Just as we need to make a distinction between listening to a feeling of desolation (such as anger) and acting upon it, we also need to make the same distinction with consolation. Even though something moves or attracts us, that does not mean it is appropriate to go out and get it. For example, we may feel consolation at the thought of our neighbor's wife (or husband), but this does not mean it is appropriate to have an affair with that person. However, we do need to listen to this movement of consolation and hear its story. Perhaps its story is that there is a problem in our own marriage that we have not faced, or that we are out of touch with a part of our own feminine (or masculine) side which this person represents. In other words, our consolation may lead us to discover what it is that we *really* want that is being masked by a want that would not truly satisfy us.

This is the dynamic of addictions, in which we substitute a substance or process (such as alcohol or overwork) for a deep inner need (such as companionship with others or self-esteem). The sign of an addiction is that an apparent consolation turns into a desolation. As Alcoholics Anonymous says, "Our solution became our problem." Although getting drunk with our friends, for example, may bring us consolation in the short run, the result in the long run may be profound desolation as our destructive behavior fuels a cycle of shame and compulsivity.

Addictions remind us that it is important to listen to both consolation and desolation, and to do so over time. Earlier we described listening to the story of our desolation in terms of Ignatius' principle of listening to the beginning, the middle and the end of interior movements. We can do the same when we listen to the story of our consolation. For example, alcohol is a good thing that can help us to celebrate. However, a recovering alcoholic knows right from the beginning that he cannot take a drink. His companion may be able to enjoy the first couple of drinks, but in the middle of the party after three or four drinks he becomes sick to his stomach. A third person may be able to drink all she wants at the beginning and in the middle, but the end result is that she is spending so much time out with her friends that her marriage is suffering. A fourth person may be able to use alcohol moderately and stop before there are any negative consequences. For this person, alcohol does not interfere with carrying out the purpose of his life. It may even help him celebrate the direction his life has taken when he throws a birthday party to give thanks for his eighty years of life.

Does the purpose of our life or our sealed orders change?

We don't think so, but our *understanding* of our sealed orders changes and evolves. For example, over the past twenty years I (Dennis) have chosen different words and phrases to describe my sealed orders, from community builder, to reconciler, to healer, to dancing heart, and lately to giving God a good reputation. Each new word or phrase doesn't cancel the previous one but rather builds upon it. Perhaps it's like an oak tree that stretches out as it grows, with each branch dividing to make new ones. Yet the tree of our life remains the same.

As I try to find direction for my life, how do I know if I'm listening to God or to myself?

As you do the examen, you are listening to both God *and* yourself, since God speaks within your deepest experience. The sign that you are listening well to this interior presence of God is if the fruits are God-like: if you are led to think and act more like Jesus. The measure of any spiritual process or movement is whether it helps us to be Jesus. For example, when the Church's inquisitors interrogated St. Joan of Arc about her visions, they said accusingly, "Your visions are just your imagination." Knowing that her visions were leading her to give and receive love as Jesus would, she defended her interior experience by saying, "Of course God is speaking through my imagination! How else would God speak to me?"

Doesn't your emphasis on listening to experience run the risk of ignoring or contradicting the wisdom of Church tradition, religious authorities, or the Bible?

Church tradition, religious authorities and the Bible are sources of divine revelation. Our life experience, as expressed through our consolation and desolation, is also a source of divine revelation. The examen can help us be open to all these sources of truth, since the examen helps us listen to all that life is saying to us. For this reason Ignatius encouraged his Jesuit theologians at the Council of Trent to do the examen each day, as a way of listening for God's truth.

Sometimes there is an apparent contradiction between what we hear as we consider these different sources of truth. In this case, we may have to live with the tension of this contradiction, waiting for a solution that hopefully brings together the truth of both sides in a creative way. However, there are times when religious authority has been wrong, such as the persecution of Jews and endorsement of slavery, the Inquisition, and the Church's response to Galileo's observations of the universe. These wrongs were corrected only as individuals followed their consciences. The Church herself, in her wisdom, has a long tradition of encouraging individual conscience, going back to Paul's public disagreement at Antioch with Peter, the first pope (Gal. 2:11-14). For example, the *Declaration on Religious Liberty* of the Vatican II documents says,

> It is through his conscience that man sees and recognizes the demands of the divine law. He is bound to follow this conscience faithfully in all his activity . . . therefore, he must not be forced to act contrary to his conscience. Nor must he be prevented from acting according to his conscience, especially in religious matters.

The beloved Cardinal John Henry Newman was an especially great defender of the right of conscience within the Church:

> Some Catholic writers dilute freedom of conscience by saying that a person is free to follow his conscience only when it is "properly formed"—meaning, it seems, only when it conforms to the views of religious authority. But Newman's description of what he meant by freedom of conscience is enlightening. Suppose, he said, in his *Letter to the Duke of Norfolk,* that the pope ordered all priests in England to give up drink or decreed that there be a lottery held in every English parish.
>
> Suppose, further, that there was a particular priest who liked a little sip of wine after dinner or felt in his heart that gambling was a sin. What was he to do? "That priest in either of these cases would commit a sin," Newman wrote, "if he obeyed the pope, whether he was right or wrong in his opinion." Newman concluded this letter with a delightful observation: "If I am obligated to bring religion into after-dinner toasts (which, indeed, does not seem quite the thing) I shall drink—to the pope, if you please—still, to conscience first, and to the pope afterwards."

Whether it is the little sip of wine that gives us consolation, or gambling that gives us desolation, as Newman suggests, one way of listening to our conscience is through the voice of consolation and desolation.

The hierarchy of the Church is responsible to represent the wisdom of two thousand years of Christian tradition, a wisdom which no one of us could recreate on our own. However, tradition is a living, evolving thing, and each of us can contribute something to its accumulated wisdom. It is precisely because individuals have followed their consciences and because the official Church has eventually listened to them that today the Church actively protects the religious liberty of Jews and other non-Christians, condemns slavery, and recently apologized for its treatment of Galileo.

When I disagree with others in my church, how do I know who is right?

Your question assumes that in situations of disagreement, one side is right and the other is wrong. That is sometimes the case. However, more often, if both sides are listening carefully, both have a piece of the truth.

For instance, the Acts of the Apostles (21:10-14) records a disagreement between Paul and Agabus in which each claims to have heard the Holy Spirit. Agabus hears the Spirit telling him that Paul will be imprisoned if he goes to Jerusalem. Thus, those who hear Agabus warn Paul not to go. But Paul responds that the same Holy Spirit told him to go to Jerusalem. Thus, at first glance it seems as if either Agabus or Paul did not really hear the Spirit. Yet both had a piece of the truth. True, as Paul said, God did want him to go to Jerusalem. But just as true, as Agabus said, Paul would be imprisoned there. It seems that God wanted Paul to be warned of his impending arrest so that, when it did happen, Paul would know that even this was foreseen by God and under God's care.

Like Paul and Agabus, people who are listening to the Spirit may hear different things. Often a resolution can be found when both sides recognize the underlying values they are trying to preserve. In the case of Paul and Agabus, the underlying value was recognizing God's abiding care. A contemporary example might be the issue of birth control. Like many Roman Catholics, we disagree with our Church's prohibition of all forms of artificial birth control. Yet we agree with the values that underlie our Church's position on this issue: the sacral nature of sexuality and of all life. We try to promote these values in our own ministry. Our hope is that as many people listen to the voice of God through inner movements of consolation and desolation and share what they hear, the whole Church will find increasingly enlightened and effective ways to realize such underlying values.

But sometimes when Christians are hearing different things, they can't even talk to each other. What do you do then?

When this happens, it is often because seemingly theological or scriptural disputes are really expressions of personal hurts or needs. In such situations, theological or scriptural debate isn't usually helpful. Rather, the story of the underlying hurts needs to be heard.

For example, in our book *Good Goats: Healing Our Image of God,* we say that God never vengefully punishes us by throwing us into hell. Ellen was guiding a retreatant who had just read this book. The retreatant, an elderly priest named Joe, walked into Ellen's office, threw our book against the wall, and said, "I hate that book. It's heresy!"

Instead of defending our theology, Ellen asked Joe to spend the rest of the retreat reflecting upon what had given him consolation and desolation in his relationship with God. Gradually the following story emerged: As a child, Joe was beaten regularly by his father. Although he appealed to other adults for help, no one ever confronted his father or intervened to protect Joe. Joe had been taught that God punishes people who hurt others, and his only consolation was the thought that someday God would avenge the beatings by sending his father to hell.

As Joe realized that his problem was not a theological disagreement with us but rather an unhealed hurt in his own life, he and Ellen began to pray for healing. As Joe experienced Jesus' healing love, his desire to punish his father diminished. He realized that his father must have also been deeply wounded in order to punish a child so severely. Joe could then feel compassion for his father, and he no longer needed an image of God as a vengeful judge who would send his father to hell.

Joe's consolation as a child had revealed a truth: that God cared about his suffering. As an adult, his consolation revealed an even deeper truth: that God cares about everyone's suffering, and that God heals suffering through love, not vengeance.

This story is an example of something we first heard from Anne Wilson Schaef. Anne said that when Christians hear something that threatens them, they often point their fingers and cry "Heresy!" as Joe did initially. When people in recovery hear something that threatens them, they are more likely to ask themselves, "What hurt or need in my own life is this triggering?" This is because people in recovery have generally learned to reflect upon their own reactions rather than blaming others.

As in the story of Joe, the examen is a means of reflection that can help us discover when an apparent disagreement is really an unhealed hurt. In this way, such situations become opportunities for compassionately giving and receiving love.

You keep talking as if God's will is always for me to give and receive more love. How do I know that? Every day I have to be in situations that drain life from me and where I don't feel able to give or receive love.

God's will is for us to be like Jesus, and for Jesus love was the norm. Jesus came to teach us how to give and receive unconditional love (Mt. 22:34–40; Jn. 13:34). God created us in such a way that we need love for spiritual, emotional and even physical health. For example, just thinking about a time when we gave or received love with another person can strengthen our immune system enough to abort a cold.

It is true that sometimes we find ourselves in situations where it is not immediately apparent that we can give and receive love. For example, we (Dennis and Sheila) have two friends who are alcoholics. When we were with this couple and they were drinking, we found it increasingly difficult to give and receive love with them. We did what we could to change the situation, including attempting an intervention. Nothing worked, and finally we told our friends that we could not be with them when they were drinking. We had realized that this was not a situation in which we could give and receive love.

Like Jesus on the cross, we may find ourselves in situations that drain life from us and where at first it seems difficult to give and receive love. We may be called to endure these situations if we sense that in the long run they will empower us to give and receive more love. However, if a situation is a constant source of desolation in which life and love are drained from us, then we need to listen to whether our desolation is guiding us to leave that situation. If we cannot leave it, we need to consider ways we can change it or protect ourselves within it.

Is this examen process for everyone, or do you have to be an emotionally mature person to benefit from it?

As we have shared earlier, even small children can do the examen. However, we do it differently at each stage of development. What gives us consolation at one stage of development may not give us consolation at a later stage of development. We may look back on decisions we made at an earlier stage and realize that we would never make the same decisions today. Yet it is only by being faithful to our experience at our current stage of development that we grow into the next stage.

According to Erik Erikson, three of the stages of psychosexual development are autonomy, play and generativity. A two-year-old at the autonomy stage may feel consolation from holding on to his or her toy. A five-year-old in the play stage may feel consolation from sharing the toy with other children. An adult in the generativity stage may feel consolation from working hard to save money to buy a toy for his or her child. The two-year-old will have difficulty growing into shared play or generative adulthood if forced to share or give away a toy before having been allowed to say "Mine!" long enough.

We doubt many people reading this book are chronologically two years old or five years old. But many of us have carried into adulthood unmet childhood needs that compromise our ability to be mature and caring adults. In fact, trying to care for others at the expense of our own needs is one definition of co-dependency. When the needs of one developmental stage are met, we naturally move on to the next stage. Because the movements of consolation and desolation reveal our needs, the examen can help us care for ourselves at our current stage of development and thus establish the foundation for moving on to the next stage and ultimately into mature adulthood.

Within adulthood itself, the examen can be an especially helpful means of growth. According to Erikson, the transitional stage into adulthood is adolescence (approximately ages twelve to eighteen) and the developmental task is identity. The examen questions of what gives consolation and desolation are a basic way of helping the adolescent discover "Who am I?"

The task of the stage of young adulthood (ages eighteen to thirty-five) is intimacy, and the examen helps us reflect on our experience of giving and receiving love with others. Moreover, when we share the examen, intimacy grows as we learn to understand others and become sensitive to what brings them consolation and desolation.

In mid-life (ages thirty-five to sixty-five), the task is generativity, i.e., generating life. People in mid-life often struggle to find the best ways to reach out and care, and to balance care for others with care for self. The examen helps us discover ways of caring that give us life rather than draining life from us.

The final stage of life is old age and the task is integrity. Integrity means we can gratefully say Yes to our own life because we can see the meaning woven through all of it. The examen's daily practice of getting in touch with what we are grateful for is the finest preparation we can think of for a fundamental attitude of gratitude in old age.

It is not important that we figure out what stage we are in, nor can we push ourselves from one stage to another. Throughout life we move back and forth between the tasks of all the eight stages of development suggested by Erikson. If each day we discover what gives us life and do more of it, we will be resolving whichever developmental task is facing us. We will naturally move on to the next developmental task by simply listening to our consolation and desolation.

I understand how God speaks through consolation and desolation to people who are holy and who pray a lot. But I'm a beginner and it's hard for me to believe God would speak to me.

The examen puts us in touch with the voice of God that is within every person. St. Ignatius discovered the examen when as a soldier who liked wine, women, and song, he was recovering from a battlefield injury in which his leg was wounded by a cannonball. To escape from his pain and boredom, he read the only two books in his castle, one on the life of Christ and the other on the lives of the saints. He also distracted himself with daydreams of continuing his life of wine, women and song at the king's court. His early experience of the examen is described as follows:

> When he was thinking of the things of the world he was filled with delight, but when afterwards he dismissed them from weariness, he was dry and dissatisfied. And when he thought of going barefoot to Jerusalem and of eating nothing but herbs and performing the other rigors he saw that the saints had performed, he was consoled, not only when he entertained these thoughts, but even after dismissing them he remained cheerful and satisfied. But he paid no attention to this, nor did he stop to weigh the difference until one day his eyes were opened a little and he began to wonder at the difference and to reflect on it, learning from experience that one kind of thoughts left him sad, the other cheerful. Thus step by step, he came to recognize the difference between the two spirits that moved him.

This examen changed Ignatius so much that he left behind his wild life and set off barefoot for Jerusalem. Because the examen was so central to his conversion and continued growth, he would teach the examen to everyone, even beginners.

The criteria for hearing the voice of God, as Ignatius did, is not "holiness," but rather the willingness to become aware. The breakthrough for Ignatius was when he moved from unawareness of his consolation and desolation to awareness, from "nor did he stop to weigh the difference" to "one day his eyes were opened a little and he began to wonder at the difference and to reflect on it." During his retreats, Anthony DeMello, S.J., used to say that a person cannot sin in awareness. We understand this to mean that God is always speaking within us, and the more aware we become, the better chance we have of hearing God's voice. (By awareness we mean not only mental cognizance but also, as in the case of Ignatius, an affective "intouchness" in which we really take in what we are feeling.) The examen helps us hear the voice of God because, in paying attention to consolation and desolation, we become aware.

What if I run into more difficulties you haven't answered here?

You will. You don't have to find all your answers in a book. Your answers are inside you. You can do your examen over whatever difficulty you have, and each day let your consolation and desolation share their wisdom with you.

Examen of This Book

In any given year we read many books but benefit from only a handful. The books we benefit most from are those that move us to ask the question: What from this book do I want to incorporate into my life?

As you have probably discovered by now, an examen can be made over anything, even the reading of a book. After you have finished this book and done the examen process, you may want to ask yourself: What seems life-giving about the practice of the examen for you and what doesn't? With those answers in mind, you may want to construct your own way of doing the examen. Then you too can sleep with bread.

Notes

Pages 10-11

The way in which our unconscious continues to work on problems for us while we sleep seems to us an example of how creativity works:

> Abraham Maslow, a psychologist who studied creative people, showed that the creative process always involves a fallow moment, a still moment, when you're not trying, and you open up; you ask earnestly and then you let go. And then something pops in that's bigger than anything logic can give you, and sometimes it delivers information that never existed before. It's a process of using the hemisphere of the brain where music comes from. (Patricia Sun, quoted in Michael Toms, *At the Leading Edge* [Burdett, NY: Larson Publications, 1991], 264.)

Thus, doing the examen before we go to sleep not only allows our unconscious to be bathed in the gratitude we feel from whatever gave us consolation, but it also allows a "fallow moment." The creativity of this fallow moment can reveal new possibilities for whatever gave us consolation and send help for whatever gave us desolation. This is why even a few minutes spent on the examen each day can be so fruitful. In those few minutes we can "open up" and then "let go" and let the mysterious realm of the unconscious do its work.

This mysterious realm, the realm that gives rise to creativity and to music, is also the realm where intuitions and premonitions come from. We are learning from the science of parapsychology that all of us have a capacity for extrasensory perception, as when a mother "knows" that her child is in danger and runs to the backyard just in time to save him from drowning in the swimming pool. That mother's "knowing" was most likely a feeling of desolation, such as a sick feeling in the pit of her stomach or a wave of a terror in her chest. Thus, attending to our consolation and desolation can open us to sources of help and guidance that our rational, conscious minds are likely to overlook.

Page 15

Anne Wilson Schaef, *Co-Dependence* (Minneapolis: Winston Press, 1986), 59.

The discoveries of psychosomatic medicine have taught us that using the examen to help us trust our needs and desires can bring not only emotional health but also physical health. For example, Dr. Bernie Siegel writes,

> In the latest article I've read by Dr. Solomon (Henry Dreher, "A Conversation with George Solomon," *Advances: Journal of the Institute for the Advancement of Health,* 5(1), 1988) . . . he says there is one simple question AIDS patients can ask themselves to gauge their chances of long-term survival: Would you do a favor *you didn't really want to do* for a friend who asked you to? If the answer is no, according to Solomon, that has more positive significance in predicting long-term survival than any of the elaborate lists of personality characteristics they have been able to develop. At my lectures, I tell audiences to imagine that they have AIDS or cancer and only six months to live. A friend calls to ask a favor on a day when they have a wonderful activity planned. Would they say yes or no to their friend? I find that less than half, and sometimes as few as 10 or 20%, say that they would respond with a no; but the people at patient workshops are much more likely to say no, which indicates to me that those who choose to attend such gatherings have already learned a lot about survival. (Bernie Siegel, MD, *Peace, Love & Healing* [New York: Harper, 1989], 162–63)

Thus, a helpful variation of "What am I most grateful for and what am I least grateful for?" might be, "What am I doing because I enjoy it and what am I doing because I should?"

Page 17

In addition to the examen, there are other ways to make decisions that we may also want to use, especially when the decision is a serious one. These include asking what Jesus would do, sharing with others such as a spiritual companion and listing the pros and cons of each of our options. Ultimately, however, all these ways of discerning come back to variations on the examen question. For example, Jesus would always do whatever would bring the most life, a spiritual companion or others who love us will encourage us to do whatever will bring us the most consolation, and our pros and cons will be based upon what we expect to bring us consolation or desolation. Furthermore, our ability to effectively use any of these other means of discernment will be greater to the extent we have learned through practices such as the examen to listen to our own experience of what gives us consolation and desolation.

Page 19

Quote is from Dick Westley, *A Theology of Presence* (Mystic, CT: Twenty-Third Publications, 1988), 29, 31, 35.

Page 44

Viktor Frankl, *Man's Search for Meaning* (New York: Washington Square Press, 1963), 104.

Pages 52-54

Focusing was originally developed by Eugene Gendlin at the University of Chicago. See his book *Focusing* (New York: Bantam, 1978). We learned focusing from Peter Campbell and Edwin McMahon, who have integrated it with Christian spirituality. For an excellent brief introduction, see Peter Campbell, "Focusing: Doorway to the Body-Life of Spirit," *Creation Spirituality* (May/June, 1991), 24, 26, 27, 50, 52. For a listing of books and retreats, write Institute for Bio-Spiritual Research, P.O. Box 741137, Arvada, CO 80006-1137.

Page 57

Austin P. Flannery (Ed.), *The Documents of Vatican II,* Declaration on Religious Liberty, I.3.

Murray J. Elwood, "Newman's 'Kindly Light' Still Brightly Shines," *NCR,* June 1, 1990, 11.

Pages 59-60

Anne Wilson Schaef, "My Journey to Understanding Addictions," presentation at conference on "Recovering Intimacy," Rutland, Vermont, June 24-28, 1990.

Page 60

The study of how recalling times of giving and receiving love can strengthen our immune system was by David McClelland of Harvard Medical School. Cited in Larry Dossey, *Healing Words* (San Francisco: Harper, 1993), 109-110.

Pages 60-62

For a more thorough description of the eight stages of development according to Erikson and the critical task for each stage, see our book *Healing the Eight Stages of Life* (Mahwah, NJ: Paulist Press, 1988).

Page 62

Quote is from William J. Young, S.J. (trans.), *St. Ignatius' Own Story* (Chicago: Loyola University Press, 1980), 10.

Books

Healing Spiritual Abuse & Religious Addiction, by Matthew Linn, Sheila Fabricant Linn and Dennis Linn (Paulist Press, 1994). Why does religion help some people grow in wholeness, yet seem to make others become more rigid and stuck? Discusses religious addiction and spiritual abuse, and offers ways of healing the shame-based roots of these behaviors. Includes how spiritual abuse can also be sexually abusive, and how scripture has often been used to reinforce religious addiction and spiritual abuse. Concludes with an image of healthy religion, in which we are free to do what Jesus would do and to listen to our experience through processes like the examen.

Good Goats: Healing Our Image of God, by Dennis Linn, Sheila Fabricant Linn and Matthew Linn (Paulist Press, 1994). We become like the God we adore, and if our God is shaming and abusive we are likely to shame and abuse ourselves and/or others. One of the easiest ways to heal ourselves and our society is to heal our image of God, so that we know a God who loves us at least as much as those who love us the most. Discusses whether God throws us into hell or otherwise vengefully punishes us, and the role of free will. Includes a question and answer section that gives the theological and scriptural foundation for the main text.

Belonging: Bonds of Healing & Recovery, by Dennis Linn, Sheila Fabricant Linn and Matthew Linn (Paulist Press, 1993). Twelve Step recovery from any compulsive pattern is integrated with contemporary spirituality and psychology. Defines addiction as rooted in abuse and as our best attempt to belong to ourselves, others, God and the universe, and helps the reader discover the genius underneath every addiction.

Healing the Eight Stages of Life, by Matthew Linn, Sheila Fabricant & Dennis Linn (Paulist Press, 1988). Based on Erik Erikson's developmental system, this book helps to heal hurts and develop gifts at each stage of life, from conception through old age. Includes healing ways our image of God has been formed and deformed at each stage.

Healing of Memories, by Dennis & Matthew Linn (Paulist Press, 1974). A simple guide to inviting Jesus into our painful memories to help us forgive ourselves and others.

Healing Life's Hurts, by Dennis & Matthew Linn (Paulist Press, 1978). A more thorough book to help the reader move through hurts using the five stages of forgiveness.

Healing the Greatest Hurt, by Matthew & Dennis Linn and Sheila Fabricant (Paulist Press, 1985). Healing the deepest hurt most people experience, the loss of a loved one, through learning to give and receive love with the deceased through the Communion of Saints.

These and other books by the authors are available from Paulist Press, 997 Macarthur Blvd., Mahwah, NJ 07430, (201)825-7300, FAX (800)836-3161.

Tapes & Courses (for use alone, with a companion, or with a group)

Good Goats: Healing Our Image of God, by Dennis Linn, Sheila Fabricant Linn & Matthew Linn (Paulist Press, 1994). Two-part videotape to accompany book (see above).

Healing Our Image of God, by Dennis Linn, Sheila Fabricant & Matthew Linn (Christian Video Library, 1994). Audio tapes that may be used to accompany *Healing Spiritual Abuse & Religious Addiction* and/or *Good Goats: Healing Our Image of God.*

Healing Spiritual Abuse & Religious Addiction, by Matthew Linn, Sheila Fabricant Linn & Dennis Linn (Christian Video Library, 1994). Audio tapes to accompany book (see above).

Belonging: Healing & 12 Step Recovery, by Dennis, Sheila & Matthew Linn (Credence Cassettes, 1992). Audio or videotapes and a course guide to accompany book (see above), for use as a program of recovery.

Healing the Eight Stages of Life, by Matthew Linn, Sheila Fabricant & Dennis Linn (Paulist Press, 1991). Tapes and a course guide that can be used with book (see above) as a course in healing the life cycle. Available in video and audio versions.

Prayer Course for Healing Life's Hurts, by Matthew & Dennis Linn and Sheila Fabricant (Paulist Press, 1983). Ways to pray for personal healing that integrate physical, emotional, spiritual and social dimensions. Book includes course guide, and tapes are available in video and audio versions.

Praying with Another for Healing, by Dennis & Matthew Linn and Sheila Fabricant (Paulist Press, 1984). Guide to praying with another to heal hurts such as sexual abuse, depression, loss of a loved one, etc. Book includes course guide, and tapes are available in video and audio versions. *Healing the Greatest Hurt* (see above) may be used as supplementary reading for the last five of these sessions, which focus on healing of grief.

Dying to Live: Healing through Jesus' Seven Last Words, by Bill & Jean Carr and Dennis & Matthew Linn (Paulist Press, 1983). How the seven last words of Jesus empower us to die or to fully live the rest of our life. Tapes (available in video or audio versions) may be used with the book *Healing the Dying,* by Mary Jane, Dennis & Matthew Linn (Paulist Press, 1979).

Audio tapes for all of these courses (except *Belonging*) are available from Christian Video Library, 3914-A Michigan Ave., St. Louis, MO 63118, (314) 865-0729. *Belonging* audio tapes are available from Credence Cassettes, 115 E. Armour Blvd., Kansas City, MO 64111, (800) 444-8910.

Videotapes for all of these courses (except *Belonging*) may be purchased from Paulist Press. *Belonging* videotapes are available from Credence Cassettes (address above).

Videotapes on a Donation Basis

To borrow any of the above videotapes, contact Christian Video Library (address and telephone above).

Spanish Books & Tapes

Several of the above books and tapes are available in Spanish. For information, contact Christian Video Library.

Retreats & Conferences

For retreats and conferences by the authors on the material in this book and related topics such as healing and discernment, and on other material in the resources listed above, contact Dennis, Sheila & Matthew Linn, c/o Re-Member Ministries, 3914-A Michigan Ave., St. Louis, MO 63118, (314) 865-0729 or (303) 476-9235.

About the Authors

Dennis, Sheila and Matt Linn work together as a team, integrating physical, emotional and spiritual wholeness, having worked as hospital chaplains and therapists, and currently in leading retreats and spiritual direction. They have taught courses on healing in over forty countries and in many universities, including a course to doctors accredited by the American Medical Association. Matt and Dennis are the authors of thirteen books, the last eight co-authored with Sheila. Their books include *Healing of Memories, Healing Life's Hurts, Healing the Dying* (with Sr. Mary Jane Linn) and *To Heal As Jesus Healed* (with Barbara Shlemon Ryan), *Prayer Course for Healing Life's Hurts, Praying with Another for Healing, Healing the Greatest Hurt, Healing the Eight Stages of Life, Belonging: Bonds of Healing & Recovery, Good Goats: Healing Our Image of God* and *Healing Spiritual Abuse and Religious Addiction*. These books have sold over a million copies in English and have been translated into fifteen different languages.

About the Illustrator

Francisco Miranda lives in Mexico City. In addition to illustrating *Good Goats: Healing Our Image of God* and *Healing Spiritual Abuse & Religious Addiction,* he has also written and illustrated several children's books.

"This is a wisdom book and a much-needed one in a time that prefers to be cynical and sad. The Lord is surely with the Linns or they could not make such profound things feel so simple."
—*Richard Rohr, O.F.M.*

"This book, with its exquisite illustrations, is a finely crafted mixture of theology, psychology and honest sharing. It reveals how profound wisdom can be made available to us if we will take the time to ask ourselves two simple questions each day."
—*Drs. Susan and Arnold Mech*
Psychiatrists

"My husband, Tim, and I discover new insights about ourselves and our relationship by practicing the Linns' method of daily reflection. Each day has become a 'treasure of remembrances' to help us grow closer to each other and to God."
—*Barbara Shlemon Ryan, R.N.*

"Anyone can keep in touch with God by this clear, profound and simple method at the end of each day."
—*Barbara and Dr. Morton Kelsey*

"This book helps us understand ourselves better and learn how to make right choices. It's a wonderful book."
—*Robert Faricy, S.J.*
Professor of Spiritual Theology
Gregorian University, Rome

"A clear and concrete way of helping the reader be attentive to the movements of consolation/desolation as a guide to spiritual growth . . . a valuable aid for anyone desirous of growing spiritually."
—*Robert Sears, S.J.*
Professor of Pastoral Studies
Loyola University

"A wonderful book to help anyone seriously interested in their spiritual journey."
—*Leo Thomas, O.P.*
Institute for Christian Ministries

"While being incredibly simple and practical, *Sleeping with Bread* is psychologically and spiritually profound—and life changing. I recommend it enthusiastically."
—*Dr. Len Sperry*
Professor of Psychiatry
Medical College of Wisconsin